Kiss & Cry

Kiss & Cry

Half Past Three

Late Nights, Early Mornings, Volume 5

Sakari Lacross

Published by Sakari Lacross, 2021.

HALF PAST THREE

First edition. January 29, 2021.

ISBN: 979-8223466109

Written by Sakari Lacross.

Table of Contents

Poem # 1

Watch me hug you by the legs

I'm worthless without you

Sleep on your back thighs

I'm already dreaming, before I close my eyes

I feel you, playing in my dyed hair

Bright colored, short strands

I'll miss this.

I'll miss this, if you ever found a reason

To take yourself, away from me

I'd Be By Myself, Without You ~ Sakari

Poem # 2

You make me feel like I need you

Even when I'm used to

Not having anyone...

A Bird Beside A Plane ~ Sakari

Poem # 3

When you know your heart is going to be broken, why do you still stay?

When you feel another women's presence, before I do, why not exit?

I don't wanna not forgive myself, for shaming your time with me

When you know love is returned, with limitations, why do you shadow me?

How Could I Hurt The One That Loves Me? ~ Sakari

Poem # 4

I finally got to do, what I wanted to do

I finally got to pull you close

By the living room fire...

Can You Stay Over, For Several Nights ~ Sakari

I finally got to do, what I wanted to do

Poem # 5

I can take you to the darkest park

Near Michigan

And set off fireworks, at night

Once I Finally Get Your Time ~ Sakari

Poem # 6

And I believed your kiss

I believed my feelings

I believed our seconds

I believed our minutes

I believed what you showed me

I really, really, really, believed in the undiversed aftermath, in your pupils

I believed in the fortunes, beneath your clothes

And in a perfect world, I wouldn't have been shown otherwise

In a perfect world, there is no otherwise

In a perfect, we were an undiscovered, situation

In a perfect world, no other man knew you existed, but I...

Something To Believe In ~ Sakari

Poem # 7

Your scent to my nose

My senses, take you in slow

My sense of touch, doesn't register your feel

Right away.

My gift of sight, lingers your previous actions

I'm still seeing, what you did moments ago.

I hear you in echoes, with touches of moans

Although, that might just be, what I want to hear.

What I want to taste.

The rawness of your body, directly out the shower...

Only Actions Say, How I Feel ~ Sakari

Poem # 8

The thing about my feelings towards you

I don't actually understand them.

I just want you...

Me, You, In A 1 Bedroom Hotel ~ Sakari

Poem # 9

Someone left you alone before

You shouldn't look for those people again

I've been left before as well

I found you, because I stopped looking as well

Sakari

Poem # 10

I'm a man of words, but not a man of promises

I can't promise the other end, with you

I'm someone special, let it be said by another

Though I can't build up the confidence, to disagree

I disappear in my Jean's, with my skin cloaked in my hoodie

The last girl I called baby, bought my last hoodie

Sakari

If I Had You Yesterday

Poem # 1

I carefully, pronounce your name.

In a room filled with people, I think of who to avoid

Next...

I Can't ReThrow My Heart ~ Sakari

Poem # 2

Coming back to you, as a nobody

It'll be promise breaking.

Sakari

Poem # 3

Maybe you're pulling me into the clouds

With the sky's permission

I'm just difficult, towards your light

Are Any Of Your Feelings Real, Or Not... ~ Sakari

Poem # 4

Every morning, I'd reply to your smile

Your morning hair

Your thin eyesight

More of these mornings, for me...

I Want You, In The Morning Too ~ Sakari

Poem # 5

I still feel insecure

But I wanna be with you, forever...

Sakari

Poem # 6

You help me, filter out my rage.

You help me, dominate my feelings...

I'm Blended Without You ~ Sakari

Up All Night Without You

Poem # 1

We're night trains, in Japan

Why wouldn't you want that?

Sakari

Poem # 2

As I laid with sickness in my blood

I wished for a more noble death.

As Covid strangled my lungs

I wanted nothing more, than to stand.

I've been bedridden, for over twelve days

I've never felt better, since I've realized...

Since I've realized my dream

Hasn't been snatched from me yet.

A Final, Final Request ~ Sakari

Poem # 3

I'm likely to die away from you

To not even go to the same afterlife as you

To find my way back to Heaven

And learn that you've already begun, paradise...

There is no era, where we have children

No lapse in time, where we start again

I could find you again, in this Era

Though I'd die, before you could carry my heart, the right way...

I'm Falling Through Floors Of Reality ~ Sakari

Poem # 4

Why can't I get rid of this feeling

Of being with you?

Did you mean that much

In such little time?

The Earliest Of Summer Crushes ~ Sakari

Poem # 5

I swear I sold my soul, for you to admire me

And it didn't work...

You were only supposed to notice me

Yet, you noticed a moment of me.

I was beautiful for a month

I was everything throughout thirty days

I should've been more specific, within my wish

My feelings, were treated underwhelmed...

Dare I say love interest? What does that even mean?

The demon Envy said she understood me

I thought my wishes were clear...

Envy, You Misunderstood Me... ~ Sakari

Poem # 6

Draw on my body, naked

Something more intimate

Than immediate

Sex...

Stalling With Your Company ~ Sakari

Getting Used To Not Being

25

Poem # 1

Take me to the dispensary, like everyday

I ask myself, was my time wasted, feels like everyday

Weed, video games and poetry, like everyday

Her feelings came before mine, like everyday

First in line, first, at the front of an emotional line

She's more emo than me

Put her hair in a bun

Put her hair in my hands

Hair in my face, when she's laying on top of me

Seems like everyday, she's aiming for her way

Like everyday, she's off and on depressed

Like everyday, she's sometimes bipolar

Like everyday, she needs her mental meds

What Does Real Commitment Do 4 Us ~ Sakari

Poem # 2

Maybe I forgot why you left me on my own

Maybe I forgot how you told me, how he makes you feel

Maybe nothing my friends say, effects my opinion of you...

Maybe when you touch me, I no longer think, of you touching him

Maybe I'm too sad, to appraise my heart, to anyone but you

Maybe you took advantage, of the right sorry soul, this time...

I'm Too Broken To Move Past You ~ Sakari

Poem # 3

Being in that space

Am I ever invited?

Things always seem so wrong for you

Wouldn't the world seem better, if we were to split it?

I've got you for the weekends

Family divides you, amongst the holidays

And work just seems so forced, since you've been behind

On rent...

Tell Me All Your Bad Eyes ~ Sakari

Poem # 4

Don't you get into the habit

Of leaving me

When you don't, get your way...

I Can't Always Give You, Your Way ~ Sakari

Poem # 5

The future doesn't belong to us

So why keep sleep fantasizing, of you?

I feel as if I'm giving up, way too soon

But you're a milestone, I've already lost, before...

The future has someone else in it

It just has to.

Because if you and I were destiny bound

You would know it, too...

It'll Be Another Millennium, Before You Tell Me You Love Me ~ Sakari

Poem # 6

My feelings dissolved with my tears

I've got dried up tears, upon my wrist

I knew a girl, that was once the answer

An older lady, who usually, makes me cry now

Sakari

Poem # 7

Pull me away

With just words

I'll understand later

That they were just words

Her Lies, Help Me Escape ~ Sakari

Poem # 8

You defend him

Like I should, defend my heart

My offensive approach

Doesn't result, in the best defense

Sakari

Poem # 9

Take my pen for once

And write our outcome

From your perspective...

In Your Own Little Way ~ Sakari

Poem # 10

That girl's the one, tearing me apart

And no, you can't have her

Sakari

Poem # 11

We dated for five days

And then broke up

Things seemed better

When I weren't, as attached

Flipped your body over

Sideways sex

Weed vape afterwards

I need someone else, to lust after

Girls Make Me Chase, Other Girls ~ Sakari

Poem # 12

Everything is in the air

Because all we do, is break up

Instead of talk

We Don't Talk Enough ~ Sakari

Poem # 13

So much on my mind right now

I can't make you a priority

Even though, I want to

I Don't Mean For Everytime, Not To Be, The Right Time ~ Sakari

Poem # 14

You've got an angel on your shoulder

I've got a demon in my prayers

I've never met, an angel before.

You've got the college, and your books

I've got drug addicted friends

Where do you and I, meet at?

I Missed Out On Normal Things ~ Sakari

Poem # 15

I've known luck...

I've known blessings...

I've known limitations...

I've known you...

I've known struggles...

I've known shame....

I've known embarrassment...

I've known you...

Before The End Of An Era (PT.1) ~ Sakari

Poem # 16

I wanna go somewhere, where it rains a lot

Somewhere, I know, you won't bother, to go...

In A City, That Stays Moist ~ Sakari

Poem # 17

When you're only living...

Is it better to die?

When dying becomes too curious...

Is it better to live?

Are our purposes only for one...

And not meant for two?

Does two always mean commitment...

When it comes down to life?

You've Made Me Feel Time ~ Sakari

Poem # 18

Point your heartbreak bullet

Towards my heart.

I wouldn't feel a thing...

Kill Me, My Crush. During Another Sunset ~ Sakari

Poem # 19

Let's always direct your hands onto the wall

Instead of on me

Always pack an overnight bag

For when you come and see me

Let's always make it seem like we're so much more

Since we've got history

Always turn your bra-less back to me

When you're laying, so close to me

Morning In Japan ~ Sakari

Poem # 20

If it's different, then it's different.

I guess I'm the one...acting different.

Those lame people in your background

Looking for a reaction

You allow them, to tear us further

You allow them, in your head

I can bet on my grandmother's grave...

And on my children's grave...

You look at me, and reminisce

On everything, they say...

I'm Cold, With Family Around ~ Sakari

Poem # 21

Though we don't talk, you're still, my humming bird

Though you're on, the tip of his tongue, I can hear your humming, around my house still

I bet you choke on him now...

Three parts, I feel I've been divided to

Drinking, smoking and vibing

Where does it end...

These girls don't end.

I wanna soul search, I wanna resist

She smiles in my face...I give in

She gives me her name, she gives me her number

She gives me her time, she makes me a promise

She gives me her address, she gives me a time slot

From one to six, the morning doesn't come

She gives me her body, and I give in...

I'm Just Used To Newcomings ~ Sakari

Poem # 22

I settled down...

I settled down, with you on my lap...

Picked me up, from off the streets...

I was living, from couch to couch

But you still, had eyes for me...

I just knew, you would make me better...

With a twist of fate, you asked me, on a date

And I still have your text messages...

I'm still less alone...

I'm still thinking about the ones, that laughed at me...

Better than before, I guess

I don't appreciate you staying around, I guess

Always in my past life, I know

I need to get you home, I need to take that bus ride

To your job tonight...

I know, all of this...

Sad for me, like a funeral

Sad for me, like you really know

You've always been a pretty girl, don't talk to me

About dark times

I can't make beautiful, out of ugly

If I looked like, half the guys that girls crush on

I wouldn't be, in dark times...

Dark Times PT.2 ~ Sakari

Poem # 23

Chill guitar beats, with my coffee, in my hand

A notebook to accompany, and your picture on my phone, to accommodate

The mood is already straight.

Stressless afternoon, for once, in so many afternoons

No work tomorrow

I'm free, this afternoon.

This Afternoon Will Feel Different ~ Sakari

Poem # 24

I'll never be interested in anyone

More than you

Ever, again...

Sakari

Poem # 25

I can live without most things

Though I'm still trying to figure out

How to live, without you

Am I Just Stubborn ~ Sakari

Poem # 26

I wanna stay

In touch with your soul

When your body

Is no longer available

Sakari

Poem # 27

Her family treated me

Like family should

Her family treated me

Like my family, never did

Sakari

Poem # 28

My funeral gonna be lonely

Don't nobody love me...

Sakari

My funeral gonna be lonely

Poem # 29

I'm only good at hurting you...

Making you want to hurt yourself....

Forcing you, into bad decisions...

Because you're thinking, from your emotions...

I'm No Better Than Your Next ~ Sakari

Poem # 30

You never judged my pockets

When those other girls, used to laugh at me

Desire, used to laugh at me

In high school, her and her friends, would laugh at me

Seeing as she had the perfect guy, with a perfect smile, and his parent's car

Pretty girl, she was

Even prettier, in her boyfriend's car

Career in my back pocket, part time job, I wasn't going for that

Different girls, would want me still

Then want my friends, I wasn't going for that

I wasn't born for labor

Breaking me down, while my heart's in construction

I picked up, a pen instead

While she picked up, someone else instead...

Still In Those Dark Times ~ Sakari

Poem # 31

Has ever a day past, when I haven't, thought about you?

I ask myself these things, as calendars dispose

You were my promise, of hope

And now I hope, for less chaos, within my heart.

This fire for you, and ice from your departure

When you return, you won't see much left, of the old me

Hello Chaos, Ice That Never Melts ~ Sakari

Poem # 32

If I had so wished it

We could've been, in a dream

Your subconscious...and mine...

If you really wish of it

Our dreams, would always end, at the same time

Your eyes flicker...as of mine...

I Know When You Sleep ~ Sakari

Poem # 33

I always get mad

When you hurt my feelings

Instead of telling you

That you hurt my feelings...

Sakari

Hers, Mine, Forever

Poem # 1

Am I the only one

That hears you

Calling out to me...

Whispers In My DayDreams ~ Sakari

Poem # 2

I don't know

What I'm falling in love

For

Sakari

Poem # 3

My heart is divided

That's why I can't choose

I stay unfazed and undecided

Because of this...

I Didn't Dream Of The Same Girl Last Night ~ Sakari

Poem # 4

You're the second most beautiful thing

By sight.

The first being the child

We'll make...

Beauty That Strikes Twice ~ Sakari

Poem # 5

Be my friend when I need it

Stop me from falling in love, when I need it

Knowing I need you, don't treat me like

I need you

Wipe my tears with me, when I need it

Answer your phone calls, when I need it

Knowing I need you, don't treat me like

I need you

If there was someone else, that could free me

I wouldn't be trapped, only in your cage

Be Someone I Need ~ Sakari

Poem # 6

I know you would've never left me

I know you would've stayed

Stuck it out while I smoked

Back to back cigarettes outside

You would've stayed...

Sakari

Poem # 7

Paralyzed from a kiss

You kissed me, multiple times, after that

I can't feel your kisses

When I go under, anymore

I have nothing to wait for

Anymore

I can't feel you, waking me up

Why did you ever, stop waking me up?

Do Things Really Have To Change ~ Sakari

Poem # 8

If I came back for you

As friends...

Could you ever forgive me

For my departure...

I left you with doubt.

I left you with confusion.

I didn't text a word

I just stopped talking to you...completely.

Do I Deserve Your Understanding/I Hope You Understand ~ Sakari

Poem # 9

Come sit and be pretty

On my bed...

Come eat takeout and Hershey's Kisses

On my bed...

Come on over, with those tiny black shorts on

I gift you, with those tiny black shorts on

Different activities like the Seasons

Bedroom temp too low, for no certain reason

Winter chills, you're under my cover

Summer heat, we're on top of my comforts

In between that, you're wet for Spring

Clothes Fall, in between my comforts

Winter chills, you're under my cover

Summer heat, we're on top of my comforts

All year round, over the weekend

The temperatures change, because of how I'm thinking...

Sex Like Seasons ~ Sakari

Poem # 10

I never judged you

Off your experiences

I did all the work

Anyway....

And anyway, you were stretched across the bed

Stomach first, no experience needed

Anyway, I touched across you

With patience.

I took other courses of action, from every glance behind you

That you give me...

I Treated You, Like You Were Worth The Wait ~ Sakari

Poem # 11

Rosey....

And those lips...

Instagram...

And those pics...

I really shouldn't be on Instagram

I'm supposed to be, finding myself

How is it that I found you

And I feel like, I found something, much better...

I Don't Need Anymore, Soul Searching ~ Sakari

Poem # 12

You were one of the ones

Who enjoyed my lust

One of the ones

Who offered me lust, first

We were on the same page

From the start

We just never got to experience

This lust, in your sheets...

Sakari

Poem # 13

I want to be accepted

But...

I wanna be special, in her eyes

I want to surprise her.

Force her...

To recalculate, her plans

I Cannot Envision Our Affection, So I Ask Of You... ~ Sakari

Poem # 14

Your soul must look like a parallel valley

Of sky and clouds

Something worth, an endless sleep

Your wonders, must not last long

A sky, underneath your feet

This must be your subconscious

I saw into your soul once

And I couldn't believe my eyes

You're Beautiful, On The Inside ~ Sakari

Poem # 15

I've known laughter, that sounds like, a beautiful sleep

I've known a voice, that sounds like, a solo ballad...

I've known Once Upon A Time...

I've known you...

I've known eyes, that out match, miracles...

I've known warmth, that stays at perfect degrees...

I've known a touch, that replays when troubled...

I've known you...

The End Of An Era (PT.2) ~ Sakari

When I'm Not Cared For

Poem # 1

I just can't be happy

Even when I wanna be

I Put My Happiness, In Your Hands ~ Sakari

Poem # 2

You left me on my own before too

I just don't bring it up

Sakari

Poem # 3

I see beautiful women

And I wanna step in their light

All the time

But I've gotta focus on me...

Sakari

Poem # 4

I write everything down

Because I don't have anyone

To talk to

Sakari

Poem # 5

You've never seen me cry

But don't think, you haven't made me cry...

I Can't Open Up Much ~ Sakari

Poem # 6

I got tired of asking somebody

That I love and adore

For understanding...

I Had To Let You Go... ~ Sakari

Poem # 7

How much more do I have to give up

For you to stay by my side?

I can't live a lie

But I don't want you to leave me

I'm not looking for anyone else, at the moment...

I'm Lonely, Angry, & Sad, Whose There For Me, If You're Not ~ Sakari

Poem # 8

Covid in my body

Covid in my breathing

My mother thought, Covid was gonna kill me

Text messages say she need me

But I don't need me

And I don't want me

Like Covid does...

Until Covid Leaves My Lungs/My Mama's Scare ~ Sakari

Love Must Feel Like

Poem # 1

And when I had no one else to turn to

You hugged me, from behind...

When Everyone Else Told Me No... ~ Sakari

Poem # 2

The only way to pull you in

Is to hold on to you.

I've been released you

Into his arms...

Sakari

Poem # 3

Same old sentences

Can't take you serious

I knew a girl like you

A girl that was only months, before you

Same way I looked at her

I look at you

Top floor emotions

We took the elevator, when we were in love

Sakari

Poem # 4

If you say I go, I go

If you say you love, I love

If you're under the weather, I'm soaked as well

Kind of a feeling...you and I, are a hunch.

If I Think Too Deep Into Us... ~ Sakari

Poem # 5

As long as I had you, I should've been happy

Yet, I desired, a better life

You Seem Appreciated, Without Me ~ Sakari

Poem # 6

I want you to know, everything I feel...

Everything, I'm thinking....

You're the last person

I wanna be silent with....

Sakari

Poem # 7

My feelings are cloaked

You're closer to my adore, than you think.

I'm much happier when you're around

I smile twice as much, behind your back

Sakari

Poem # 8

It's ok if you call him back

Just call me back

Right after

Sakari

Poem # 9

And after I get sad

I don't know where else to run

But by your side...

Sakari

Poem # 10

My eyes are over written

By darker energies

She speaks to me, in whispers...

Her touch is so faint.

So ghostly.

She's invisible, to those around me...

I love her in mind, she can never leave.

She traps herself there, willingly.

Willing, she wants to be, my company...

The One Girl, Who Actually Loves Me, In Spirit... ~ Sakari

My Form Of Love

Poem # 1

Drove you around my mind...

I'm ok.

Drove you around my mind...

I'm looking for a way, to express, that it's ok.

You never called our sex, anything but "Love Making"

You never let me go without my addictions

You never gave me advice, you just gave me permission

I felt like you gave me purpose, was it on purpose?

Drove you around my mind

Did you enjoy the night ride?

Drove you around my mind

Were my thoughts too vivid for you?

I've been feeling insecure, I could never imagine

Your lips against my neck tat, what was really happening?

I'm doing everything right, let you tell it

I did everything right, but you still made me

Regret it

Left me for your ex, does that make me, another ex?

My Mind Was Your Road ~ Sakari

Poem # 2

I always chicken out

When I get into these hotel rooms

With these other women

I always think, about what you'd say...

How do you do it?

How do you push forward

Letting another man, touch on you

Even when you say, you still love me...

Your Image, Comes To Mind ~ Sakari

Poem # 3

She keeps me sane

I talk to her, the entire time

She's at work

Sakari

Poem # 4

I found a mountain to climb

Hopefully, it reaches your heights.

What you seek...

What you feel...

What you acquire...

Your list of demands,

May I reach them?

Sakari

Poem # 5

In advance I crush on you

Red haired allure

You've given me, red vision

These heart eyes in person

They give me red vision

I see you, envisioned

Involved into my work...

Involve Yourself, Into My Art ~ Sakari

Poem # 6

Come back, when you get back, from Cali

Barely even knowing this dude, and he's got you, leaving state

Acting like the two of you, are together

And you say you're not

Showing me all his messages, and it's not adding up

Why do you keep letting him, call you his boo?

You only like him, because I like her

You only text him, because you see me, texting her

We're only having sex, because you're not, in Cali yet

We're only not together, because I can't put you and I, together anymore

Games With My Ex ~ Sakari

Poem # 7

When I said goodbye

It was because I was telling someone else

Good morning.

I shouldn't have treated you

Like an eternal Goodnight.

All Of Your Bad Nights... ~ Sakari

Poem # 8

It's okay. Just go. He can do more for you...

I'm just a dream chaser

I chased you, didn't I?

Now I chase an impossible path

A career, as a writer.

These things take time...

You don't have time.

You need a roof.

A guy with stable income.

A partner, without excuses.

A friend when you need him.

Valuables, to keep up to date.

Someone, who can buy you gifts, for special occasions.

Someone, who can show you, your worth. Sooner than later.

The Same Conversation, Only A Different Girl ~ Sakari

Poem # 9

Give me some kids of my own

And watch me appreciate them, as I do yours

Lay down, lay down, and lay down again

Until we make...a mini you...

Make Me A Winter Child ~ Sakari

Poem # 10

As long as you live

I'll take care of myself

After you die

I'll die Seasons apart

Life doesn't make sense without you...

Sakari

Poem # 11

I'd pay, any price of darkness

To become the shadow

In your light.

Allow the darkness

To trick me into devotion

And feel you hold me

For the first time.

I'd never wake up

From this fear...

I Cannot Always Share Your Light ~ Sakari

This Has To Be

Poem # 1

Sit on my lips first

Like you planned to do

Go ahead, make your enjoyment first

Like we've planned for you

The Night You Finally Came Over ~ Sakari

Poem # 2

As eye gazing, as you are

Am I to believe

That you cannot stop the rain

Simply, by smiling...

You do it well. You take naturals, into your blemish

All too well

There is no need, for my imagination

I'd start a cult, in your name...

Nothing happened. I saw you, and instantly grew up

I knew what had to be done.

I wanted to give you, a world without war

A domain with gems, underneath your feet

Air, that you could walk on

Puppies, that stayed puppies

I wanted to be, more grateful

Than any mortal, around your existence...

Summon Only Me, By Your Side ~ Sakari

Poem # 3

I never thought about, being your only guy

Just come over...

Sakari

Poem # 4

Talk to me.

Because I'm only twenty-eight

And I have no plans

Of slowing down.

Press me like you wanna...

Lay against me, like you wanna...

Take up my nights, like you wanna...

Give up your afternoons, like you wanna...

Let's Make Time, For More Sex ~ Sakari

Poem # 5

You've brainwashed me.

Every since your cum, bursted into my mouth

The only taste I enjoy, is your body's juice.

I'm unable to refuse.

When you lay at the edge of the bed

Legs spread, I hold them away for you

My tongue dips.

Slips, flickers, and rattles

My tongue sticks right into

Your juice squeezer

Rub my head, at the edge of your bed

Legs spread, at the edge of your bed

Halfway, off the bed

I need for you, to stay put.

Tingles, ride me lips

Your wet lips, ride my lips

Like the other thing, you would ride

Move against, my mouth and ride

Cum, sitting on my tongue

I feel your throbs

Your walls

Have my tongue surrounded.

So thick and moist

I'm so used to the taste

You call it creamy

I can't wait, for you to relax again.

So I don't wait. For you, to shower again

I catch you at the bathroom door

Where are you, going again?

Back on my knees, I've got you, standing over me

Pressed against your fresh skin

I'm sucking in between, lips again.

With clear juices, down my chin

I remember this feeling, and I snap out of it, again

Looking up at you, I realize

You're already, done again

I've been brainwashed, by your night and tales

All over again...

Rub my head, at the edge of your bed

Legs spread, at the edge of your bed

Halfway, off the bed

I need for you, to stay put.

Tingles, ride me lips

Your wet lips, ride my lips

Like the other thing, you would ride

Move against, my mouth and ride

I can't wait, for the next time

I can't wait, for the next time

I can't wait, for the next time

I can't wait, for the next time

Edge Of The Bed ~ Sakari

Poem # 6

We were outside, in your car

That wasn't enough, excitement for you

So went into the slide, at the park

After hours, we're ongoing, creativity...

Places For You ~ Sakari

Poem # 7

You left your panties here

Come back and get them

Tomorrow night...

See You Again ~ Sakari

Poem # 8

I beat sleep for you

I ignore people for you

I'm all too grateful for you

I am nothing, without my art...

I have two loves, my art and a girl

A girl in my living room, and my art, in my room

I write you

On Saturday afternoons

I am nothing, without my art...

Poetry and fiction

Lust within two fantasies

I escape reality, because of you

I'm all too grateful for you

I am nothing, without my art...

I Am Your Nothing ~ Sakari

Poem # 9

From when I first saw you, walk into the store

You couldn't imagine, the things I was thinking.

From when you looked back at me, catching a piece of my glance

I couldn't imagine, what your smile meant.

Store Run ~ Sakari

Poem # 10

I can only treat

One girl right

That's why I'll never

Cheat on you

Sakari

Sometimes, I Adore

Poem # 1

Looking at you from your pics

Like your clothes, are see through

Looking at your soul

Like your body, is see through

Reflection in your eyes

Whose else

Is in love with their phone

Because of you

24hrs In London ~ Sakari

Poem # 2

We were in high school

In my dream

I wrote you a love letter,

And we had lunch,

Together.

I met you in the parking lot

In my dream

You told me, you adore sunrise walks

And quiet places

In my dream.

Last Night's Dream ~ Sakari

Poem # 3

Later...we'll think about, each other

As of now, we're thinking about, our significant other

But how significant are they

If we can go forward, without the other?

Maybe U & I, Are More Significant ~ Sakari

Poem # 4

That sex that feels like

You're testing me

This time...I've studied...

That sex that feels like

You're broken hearted

Im sweatin, repairing it...

That sex that feels like

We're in love

Wake up Love, we're in lust...

When Spring Feels Like Winter ~ Sakari

Poem # 5

Her hurt feels so familiar

That's why I find myself

Wrapped in her comforts

Let's Get Better Together ~ Sakari

Poem # 6

I'm not good

With one night stands

I still haven't grasped, the concept yet

I give you sex

Then a cooked meal.

We hold hands and watch TV, in the bed

Then sex again.

I wake you up, around 6AM

But you don't have to go home.

More sex

And then we lay up

We watch the sunrise

Breakfast in bed, about an hour away

I still haven't grasped, the concept yet

More Than A Night ~ Sakari

Poem # 7

I can be your man

Though we'd only be built

Off sex...

I can be your man

Liquid legs, every night

And that's it...

Sakari

Poem # 8

I'm not sure

How much in love with you

He actually is.

So when you see me

Just walk

Right past me...

Our Only Secret ~ Sakari

Poem # 9

Maybe I remember, too much

Maybe I didn't forget, anything, at all...

I Remember Her Feel ~ Sakari

Poem # 10

When she calls me cute, because I'm 5 foot 5

When she calls me, after only four hours of sleep

When she calls me, as if, I'm her only contact

When her long distance voice, feels like company

She Became When I... ~ Sakari

Poem # 11

We shall cover up the moon

With your naked image

I see you on top of me

And the moon's image, behind you

This Night ~ Sakari

Don't miss out!

Visit the website below and you can sign up to receive emails whenever Sakari Lacross publishes a new book. There's no charge and no obligation.

https://books2read.com/r/B-A-GXQL-IWULB

Also by Sakari Lacross

Endless Journal
Wherever You Might Be
Something Else To Hurt About
Something Else Entirely
I Once Had A Heart
Mood
Another Mood
Patient Hearts
Never Ending
Unspoken Words
The Realm In Between

Eternal Flames
Burn Brothers

Fantasia's Dream
Fantasia's Dream

Hashtags
Hashtags

How Long Is Forever
How Long Is Forever
How Long Is Forever
How Long Is Forever

Late Nights, Early Mornings
3 AM Thoughts
4 AM Thoughts
5 AM Thoughts
6 am
Half Past Three
2am Worries
1am Loner
Midnight Talks

Lyrics
Lyrics

Mental Health
PTSD
Anxiety

Schizophrenic

My Soul Mate
The Only Girl I Really Want

Perfect Gentleman
Perfect Gentleman

Sunset Szn
Sunset Szn
Sunset SZN 2
Sunset SZN 3

This Is For Her
Someone Like You
Someone Like You Too
Someone Else Like You

Standalone
The Legend Of Krampus

About the Author

Michael Wayne Noland Jr, better known for his pen name Sakari Lacross, was born February 5th, 1994 in Cleveland Ohio. Spending most of his childhood being raised in Flint Michigan, Michael's mother moved him and his family to Arizona when he was 15. Even with his unstable background, Michael has been writing since he was nine years old, competing in his school's poetry contest and bimonthly writing events. Discovering all his true potential to write during his years he went to linden charter academy, Michael won his first local poetry contest at Sam Garcia Western Avenue Library, located in Avondale Arizona. Michael then published his first poetry collection, titled, PTSD. With so many more projects on the way, Michael has no plans of stopping his love for writing any time soon and encourages his readers to stick around for the rides to come.